Last Man Standing

Poems for my Father

Stuart Medland

AGENDA EDITIONS

ISBN 978-1-908527-16-5

First published in 2014 by
Agenda Editions, The Wheelwrights
Fletching Street, Mayfield
East Sussex, TN20 6TL

Design and production by JAC design
Crowborough, East Sussex

Printed and bound in Great Britain by
TJ International Ltd, Padstow, Cornwall

Contents

One

Centrifugal	8
On Oath	9
Shopping Trolley	10
The Cheese gave it Away	11
Nearly Tea-time	12
Joke	13
Guilt-edged	14
Last Man Standing	15
Renault Megan	16

Two

Small Breaths	18
Talking us Through	19
Line of Sight	20
Tug of War	21
Sleep at All	22
On Parade	24
Bedtime	25
Careful with Bones	27
Nil Points	28
Bearhug	29
Under the Sun	30
Big Hand	31
Keeping Still	32
Last Grand Prix	33
Dad's Weeds	34
Quietus	35
Miles	36
Meaning Something	38
This Man	39
The Force in May	40
Double Take	41
At the Church of St. James at St. Kew	42

Three

Ford	46
Odd Chorister	48
To St. Tudy	49
Hard Done By	50
On the Promenade at Margate	52
The Photo in the Drawer	53
The Wrestling Field	54
Jack	55
Circle for a Maid	56
Lol	57

Four

Demob	60
One Moment	61
All	62
Point Duty	63
Garages	64
In Red	65
Fingerprints	66
My Dad's a Policeman	67
Half an Ounce of Old Holborn	68
Cornwall	70
Pickled Onions	72
On Sweltering Days	73
At the Crease	74
Night Fishing	75
How Men Run	77
Still Life with Apples	79
Stand Up Straight	80
Dave Allen	81
People	82
The Sniff	83
Playing Table Tennis	84
Nine Card Brag	85
A Certain Age	86
Out on a Limb	89
Blackberries	90
Company Man	91
Shallows	93
Four Sons	94
Creases	95
Toughening Up	96

One

Centrifugal

When you first saw the scan –
Your body betrayed
through its own eyes –

And the cancer, blackberries
dung-beetle rolling
to take their turn with
every cell of every bone,

How did you not
curl up in one corner of the bathroom
with the door locked and your
arms locked over your head?

I wonder

If you haven't always
let the whirl of devastations
flatten out your breath
against the wall – been

Centrifugal – out at the very

Edges of our sight.

On Oath

Why did you put yourself
On Oath to say
nothing at all to begin?
Was it in case we
might use it against you?
Use what, exactly?

When were you going to give us
the time that we needed?
That's right – we. Not
You, exclusively.

Where is the weakness
in the telling of a
violation? Oh,
but you should know.

What muddy-puddle reservoir
or Marianas Trench of
inner fortitude was it
you hoped to draw upon
by not so doing?

Strong and silent type.

Shopping Trolley

I couldn't tell
if you were leaning on the
supermarket trolley outside Safeways
with a sudden stitch

Or if your back
was playing-up
(as it was prone to do
when we were small
enough for rough-
and-tumble games but
old enough to recognise
that sharp intake of
breath and both desist a
pop-eyed second).

Why the candle-moth concern
of those who lately knew you well,
for such a twinge? The whispered-looks
that queried whether this was
such a good idea? What was it

That I didn't know? And why the
storm-cloud face that had me wondering
what indiscretion lay within my noticing you

Wrestling with the trolley wheels

Like everybody else?

The Cheese gave it Away

I caught you smarting.

It was when you brought your Cornish weight down
on the flagstone cheddar – making us our
cheese and onion sandwiches.

'Dad? What's the matter with your arm?' I asked you.

'Arm? What arm? What do you mean, my arm?'
you flashed at me and
made the breadcrumbs pay
by sweeping them into the sink.

I should have known, of course,

The cheese was stale, the
onions far too strong and

You are never ill.

Nearly Tea-time

In a daytime space, between
one cup of tea and another,
before people come home from
work and from school – such
ordinary things – I have
picked up the phone and
am still trying to believe
what it took upon itself
to tell me. Whatever

It was, the two of us have
tripped-up and stumbled our
separate ways to a wordless sob
which has lodged itself, now,
as an ache at the back of the throat –

Swallowing nothing.

Soon, the first words must bob to the
surface of these slow-swimming eyes,

While my white-knuckle fist
crushes this, whole.

Joke

Your bones have run riot.
The cells of them
Have lost their heads –

Are caving you
Outside in. They are
Inciting a pain that

Leads you around
Like a big-hearted bull
With a ring through

Its nose. You have to
Follow, hostage,
Hoping to negotiate –

Softly, softly
And sharing the joke –

Your own release.

Guilt-edged

I felt I was betraying you
by always telling family so far away
that you were looking older
than the last time that I saw you;

All your thick, black Brylcreem hair
like wisps of smoke now, at the door,

Your feet in manacles of shuffles and
your nut-brown skin entirely
melted, pale and loose, yet

Hooked up on a smile
to let me in –

So they would come.
before it was too late.

Last Man Standing

We cannot stop you
Decorating – Forth
Bridge – always
doing-up the house.

Invest enough of
yourself in the house
and it'll fall down
before you do.

I find you stripping wallpaper –

Standing in a pile of
soggy front-room peel.
'Look at that lot! It's
remarkable what you can do
with one good arm in
the space of a morning' –
you announce, with
only half a flourish.

I think, 'you've changed your
tune since the cheese.'

I come across you
painting the banisters,
left-handed, frowning back up
at the top of the stairs with
not wanting them to dry when
I arrive next time; your
skin as clammy as
wallpaper-paste,
beaded with night
condensation,

Popping with water
straight from your forehead
with being the Last Man Standing,

With being afraid to sit down.

Renault Megan

You'd set your heart
on a Renault Megan;

The Motorbility Allowance
might just run to one of those.
You fancied that. Converted
at the garage to defer to your
one-handedness. You

Could be sporty on the road –
(despite a compromise
to do with handbrake turns)
in lieu of having not been
born as Graham Hill – a
big mistake on Someone's part.
Yes, British Racing Green it
could be. Just the job.

Instead, they offered you
a Clio for the weekly
shopping – and to
pootle round the block.

Two

Small Breaths

Your pain inhabits you –
believes it has a
right to you by now.

You are taking
small breaths
to hold the pain in
Rizla-paper-thin
between them

So it does not
have the room
to turn and turn and
make itself at home.

Talking us Through

Already, you are
talking us through –

Making it easier for us.
Painting your illness
by numbers. We nod.

We are trying to follow the
plan, the roadmap,
the blueprint;

Whatever it is
you must have been
given. Our

Thoughts of you are
regular as heartbeats now.

Suddenly – Life
is a bolthole
we are, all of us,

Crowding for at once.

Line of Sight

You hold onto things
such as words, for their
semblance of weight

But if they slip away
to the edge of our talking,
you do not look to follow.

The wind is flapping rain
against the glass. I watch you
frowning through it, only

Allowing your mind
to travel along your line of sight.

I am gathering news,
making-up news, even,

To keep the words running –
like marbles from a child's own
kitchen-roll chute,

Clinking and bright,
across the table –

All along your line of sight.

Tug of War

You let your strength go
only bit by bit, let it out
a little at a time –

Knowing it is only right
to exact a price
for your trouble

Like a man at a tug-of-war
who is burning his hands
on the rope,
ploughing furrows
with his heels
across a field of turf
to lock himself

Against the weight
of carthorses, of life-
boats loosed – unstoppable,
on slipways. You have
no equal and opposite
momentum of your own.
Others wrap the rope
around your waist –

To make it pay
for every inch.
And still

You do not talk
of unfair sides.

Sleep at All

This time

Your eyes filled to the brim
as I came in –
that I should see you like this
with the legs that fold away
as easily as the wheelchair – spilled

As your new weakness shook you.

It is all still such a long surprise.

You blink at the blank of the window,
working-up a squeaky smile against the glass
before you turn. I joke
of only having come
to watch the football on tv.
Your smile is caught in your face
as if it was a baseball glove. You

Roll a feeble weed, stretching
for the bits you need – and for the sake of company allow the
'Yes, he's looking better than he has done.
Yesterday was bad. He gets upset sometimes' –
As if your pain means you're no longer one of us,
not quite a grown-up any more because
you speak a simpler language now. Once

Mary found you, shaking to yourself in
a room you weren't sure of, your back to the doorway and
frightened (at last) that you might have been left on your own.

We slide and we shift you across
(it is like a pantomime) from the
chair-to-keep-you-upright to the chair
we need to leave you in alone with your new ignominy, while
remembering to bring your feet along with us. *'Oh, look'* –
You observe, in a small amusement of disbelief,
'I'm like a puppet. Where are my strings?'

You take the photograph of Col and Dan
at once with both big hands, as if it did in fact
contain them – was a lifeline you might
turn and squarely turn to reel them in –
a stopcock that might open up the way back to a
time when you were far too young to be a
Gramps and not too pleased about it. All

This afternoon there have been mewings
in your throat that you seem not to be responsible for
yet have nonetheless adopted you.

*

You sit at the front door, querying the orange-
glow dark of the street, pushed to the brink of the drive
by only guessed-at hands and by the light behind you
all the way back up the hall. You've come
to see me to the car. Your hand

Takes shaky leave of the wheelchair arm to wave.
(They are going to fit a ramp next week so you
can sit out in the sun.) Your whole face quivers.
You will smile at me until I'm gone
if it's the last thing that you do.

I'll drive to the end of the road
and turn to come back down again.

Tomorrow I'll have kept this promise.
You will tell me you have had the
best night's sleep you can remember.

I will say how pleased I am – and wonder
you should ever want to sleep again.

On Parade

Your only worry –
your one small panic
is that your feet
might not be together.
'Are my feet together?'
You ask,
whenever we move you.
'Are they?'
As if you don't want them

Untidy for anyone. As
if, after a lifetime of
making up your own way of
doing everything –
It is time to be simply

Standing up straight again.
Time to be told,
time to be

Back on parade.

Bedtime

The kind nurse
comes early
(because there are
others to visit, no doubt)
to put you to bed.

It throws you a little.
You have to be ready

Already. You
search the face of the clock
in a panic, for its time.
You search mine.

Your hands grip your
chair in a spasm of
helplessness only I
notice and still they are
too big to hold.

'Isn't it a bit too soon?'
You clear your throat
to ask her. She is busy.

(She has no idea
that you were C.I.D.
You have evidently
lost your fabled powers
of interrogation.)

You try her once again
by swivelling your head
around your crumbling
shoulder. *'Somebody –*
look – has come to
visit me today.
I mustn't go to bed
while they are here'.

She smiles. You
shake your worn-out head.

'I don't know. I don't know,'
you sigh. (The very words
you always used to
blow the World away
in your exasperation,
the rusty raffia
of a life resigned –
a muscle-jerk
scuff of the
heel in the dust.)

The nearest you came
to making a fuss.

Careful with Bones

When I hug you –
from my half-way point
with bending to your chair,

I'm careful, now, to leave your
brittlestar and chalky bones
as I have found them,
knowing I must carry all your
parting words as carefully
and fit them back together
where they now belong. I am
identifying them as if I'm
labelling each bone discovered
on an archaeological dig.

I must not break you, separate your
parting words, unwittingly.

Nil Points

There are no points to be scored,
no ends to keep up, no airs
and no graces, no stances to take, no
jockeying glances, no blame for what
might or might not have been done.

We are no longer precious or
even particular – all is reduced
to not wanting to die, not

Wanting to have

No father, no son.

Bearhug

You were a Grizzly Bear
upon your hands and knees –
A big Brown Bear we
could not ever get our
arms around enough
to hold on properly.

With my last hug
I found your other shoulder
far too readily to fit the
hollow tennis-ball of it
into my palm, to

Pull you back across the bed
to lean up straight
upon the pillow for us.

All this time you had been
slowly slipping sideways
while we chatted for your
throaty, bear-growl benefit –

And so you hadn't liked to say.

Under the Sun

My kiss upon your forehead
springs tears,

Quiet ones
that swim along your lower lid
and wobble with you –
blurring feet.

And then we talk

About everything else

That is under the Sun.

Big Hand

You hung onto your life
soon after I was born; falling
from a power station chimney
on the Isle of Grain –

Instinctively to crook an
elbow over where the
scaffolding makes cross-poles
at the corners of each plank-laid
platform, which then overlap –

On your way down.

You swung a moment with
not falling anymore –
for Mum's sake and for
several brothers yet to come –

Before you were assisted by
an Irishman who managed to
man-handle you on board and
roll you safe across his deck.
*'I wouldn't be doing that too
often, feller!'* soon

Passed into family folk-lore.

You are hanging on – and
every bit as grimly – now, while
finding a momentum that will
swing you from one day
into the next – for everybody

Who is kneeling on those
clanky planks but cannot find a
part of you to grab by which

To haul you safely back on board.

Keeping Still

You keep still – so as
not to spill one moment
of the three years
you had eked out
from the four months
you were given,

Do not waste a
single breath when
those still left to you
are counted on
our fingers now – on

Curses or on blessings

Though you stretch
your feet, I notice,
once or twice,

As if you might be
feeling for the water,
or a rope pulled tight.

Last Grand Prix

It is not like you; to be
happy to be second –
through this long
Malaysian afternoon,
.
On the tail of the leader,
(Schumacher, is it?)
for the sake of simply
going round and round
and round and round.

Content with dropping back
and being lapped by
everybody now –

Not wanting the flag
or even the points.

Dad's Weeds

Your weeds are getting everywhere;

Falling loose out of your Rizla paper
as you try to make them – thinner
and even thinner. Weeds

In your belly button
when the nurses come to wash you, weeds
in your pyjama pockets, weeds in
the crack of your bottom
when the nurses turn you over.

Weeds for this Old Holborn roll-up
made for you with dreadful –
nervous, last rites loving care,
according to an intonation
of your own instructions,

For this is the one;
The 'roll-your-own'
that you could not –
or even lick-along
to seal that flimsy
caddis tube –

Then held for you:

The lip-pinched wafer of a
damp and life-limp sacrament.

Quietus

Quietus.

Everything has stopped.

You have – and
you have gone.

This last kiss
is only placed
upon the forehead
of a cool reminder of you;

Plaster
of Paris

So soon set.

Quiet. Quit. Quietus.

Miles

I was late. Our round-trip
had turned into an oval
(a soggy ellipse, more like).
Trying to do too much.

Headlights dragged my eyes
from left to right for hours
while I thought of you
still waiting for me in the
wheelchair that gives little
scope for overtaking –
these days. It wasn't

Always so; on one occasion –
so the story goes – you'd
pulled out from behind a knock-on
crawl of cars just doing what
the rest of us are used to doing,
got it wrong and ended up
upon your back with spinning
wheels in someone's garden,
reckoned for a gonna (you
could hear them talking)
only to climb out and then
conduct your own defence
to charges brought of
Driving Without Due Care &
Attention, proving – on the
contrary – that your attention
(on the ninth car, was it?) was
uniquely riveted, your execution
of the said manoeuvre, faultless
('til the lorry came around the
bend, that is). Now, if the charge
had been of *Dangerous Driving* –
you would not have had a leg
(however useless now) to
stand upon. You drove

So far – and knackered vehicles
in the process (your due process) –
that one memorable day as you
came rolling down the drive
the engine fell out of the car.
You looked at it – and at the
Austin Maxi that it might have

Had the decency to die inside
and left it there to make a
cup of tea. It stayed there
for us all to walk around at
either end of school, a fortnight.

Four o'clock. I'd nodded off
and so I pulled into a lay-by
where I closed my eyes for
twenty minutes and then
wandered up and down
beneath the stars – not
wanting to get back
inside the car. At

Half-past four,
I learned next day,
You'd died – while I was
only such a come-and-go
commodity as miles,
as ever, from your side.

Meaning Something

It is this early in the morning. Half past four again.
Bird music is an orchestra not ready yet. A small
bat is returning home and now returning home

Another way. You are gone. You
Are gone. It must mean something.

I stand by the phone and wonder at it.
It is still the phone. The words that we have
spoken on it must be still those words.

You are still you. Though wordless now.

This Man

Had the vigour of my youth
in his late middle age, had a
gaze that could penetrate the
fumble and bluster
of a mind full of lies
and hold a hard man in it
til he bowed his head
across a table.(This man
held me in it til I spilled
more beans than strictly
necessary and he laughed
out loud).This man could

Never easily be bought
or sold. Or, notwithstanding,

Find it in him to grow old.

The Force in May

(May the force be with you)

The day you died. At some point later that same day,

It slowly dawned upon me that for some few minutes now
the whole of the Beds and Metropolitan Police Force
had been gathering outside in the road; with dogs
and thumping helicopters standing wobbly over gardens,
flack-jacketed policemen jumping out of blue and orange
stripy vans and sealing off the street. Constabulary panic –

As if somebody, who ought to know their job, had realised,
too late, that this indulgence of a Micky Mouse Retirement was
in point of fact the hard-as-nails, the cold-as-steel real thing and –
notwithstanding stable doors and horses – were now
doing what they could – dawn-raid and house-to house –
to cut off your escape. That, or

The whole wide World had lost the plot without you here.

Double Take

There had to be some mistake.

Perhaps there was a backlog of cremations
from the day before that might explain the queue
which wound around the building from the
swinging double-doors, like funeral bunting –

On the day your worlds collided, that your
double-lives colluded in your own farewell –

But no – we were expected, while my
feet and stomach went from under me
upon the dawning that these were your
workmates and the lifelong colleagues
who had known you, in their own way
just as well as we, but wholly separately.

Standing room – policemen, their own
crowd-control and women too – yet none in
uniform; your friends, who'd come, off-duty,
to see you off-duty and who knew a

Thing or two of life and death already
now collaborating with me in this – smiling,
nodding, understanding, necessarily,

You must have had a family.

At the Church of St James at St Kew

We took you back
to somewhere you knew.

You were still at large.
(You had managed two whole urns
in a carrier bag on my knees in the car
to yourself. There was a moment of
burlesque when the rector clasped his hands
and clocked his head to smile; 'whom
have we here? I see. And here?'

He took us back two hundred years, to a
stove-pipe pit on the churchyard heights,
in the big black draught of his cloak.
A man with a spade – Uriah Heep, I think –
was scraping the slate off to one side.

We stood on the slope of the hill
and could have done with
one leg longer than the other.

(I pictured myself
hauling people up the
steepness of the drive
back to the house – and
everybody buzzing with
their stories of you still.)

We found we were quiet.

It didn't quite rain.

From staring down into the earth
I must have looked up much too
quickly, blacked-out momentarily,
so when I couldn't find the
Church I knew was there
below the trees, I
tipped towards them
with a slug of vertigo – and

Missed important words. I

Concentrated on the cows to bring me back –

Watched them going in, so
slowly and inevitably, one by
one, unknowing, up the lane
to the farm at our feet.

My thinking of you
clogged in their mud;

My thinking of anything
but for the odd wish that
each of the urns contained
one of your generous ears.

Three

Ford

Here is the pebble-shiny, sixpence-clinking water
swilling thin across the road as if from buckets

At the ford – now turning muddy with the
wet earth melting from the soft stream bank and
slopping over Wellies onto socks, full-gushing up
the rubber tyres and gleamy-paint of cars come

Cleaving water noisily, while
you stand back a little, just a
little. With a stick. Still the Cornish
magic of it stirs me; that a stream
will swallow up a lane and maybe
let it go again. I've lost you in an ad-hoc
childhood of my own until I fasten

To the slap and hollow-clonk of those black
rubber Wellingtons at loose around the village,
bored of fords and aimless as a Boxing Day,
your soggy socks around your toes – jumping
halfway out of them to pull at dripping twigs
and let them spring their raindrops everywhere.

I've found the Church. I turn to hear you
running down and through the churchyard
after school, with clanging-to the kissing gate
(high on the hill as the tops of the trees) in
front of brother Keith the moment he arrives and
flying, helter-skelter, in between the gravestones,
ducking yews, with arms akimbo to be somehow
on your feet still by the bottom of the damp
and ivy-flapping tunnel slope. Stopping
at the sight of me. One

Hand upon the cold-ring iron handle
of the ship-thick, woodworm door. Caught out –
seeking a reminder of you that your Auntie Dot
had asked should never be removed; a
sticky-paper label with your name and age –
L. Medland, 8 Years – written on it, stuck
above just where, upon an ear-shaped hook
behind a stack of chairs, you hung your
choirboy surplice one last time
some sixty years ago. I watch you

backing-off on dancing feet – composure
nimbly re-asserted – and now run to

Chase the schoolcap you've just thrown ahead to
try to catch, with one look back at me before you
swing the wrought-iron churchyard gates upon
yourself and all the steps set staircase wide
to mount a lady's horse from halfway down –
another back at Keith, still catching-up, then

Quickstep down them, jumping three at once
to spot a landing on the lane and sprint,
head down, up to Trequite. Your only thoughts

Of Auntie Dot (and brother Keith, of course) and tea.

Odd Chorister

You were a choirboy here.

Under this nautical, this
treble-barrelled roof.

I slid to every space along the pew
you might have sat in, too
(and then again, might not).
I fidgeted with looking round a lot
to let my eyes decide what
might have taken your attention
from the plainsong murmuration of
a sermon going on behind you – and those
other long, long gaps between the hymns; the

Stained-glass windows colour-washing
walls and flagstones, choirboy faces,
stone-faced saints, dark-varnished angels
(winging-it like everybody else at
Viking prow and stern of choirstall pew
but nonetheless invigiliating you), a
stone-arched doorway only boys your age
would not need to bend down to
sneak away through, one verse at a
time. Did you sing up? I can remember

Only lines of happy nonsense
which you liked to make us laugh with – til
the slightest change of emphasis or tone
would have us rolling in the aisles
between the kitchen table and the chairs.

I'd no idea you had a voice
for proper singing, once upon a time

And not til even now imagined you a boy.

To St. Tudy

At barely eight years old
you were entrusted with the carthorse –
seventeen hands to your eleven, boiler-room
to your small cage of ribs. Pedestrian

Together up the nag-nod lanes; boy
riding hugely, leading now – a four-post
lumber, shadowing the lords-and-ladies
in their mossy-sunken beds. All

Earthy thuds and creaking leather,
to the blacksmith at St. Tudy
three whole miles away. You

Waited on the bench outside the forge;
the bridle passed without a Cornish word –
and but a single slap and twitch to stir a further
patient clop of hoof upon the cobbles
through the wide-flung, barn-mouth doors.

You swung your feet to scuff the dust. The
blacksmith rang his iron, heaved one
giant fetlock onto his own knee and
shifted his best foot to find a point of
balance underneath. You shifted round

To watch. Muscles passed a shiver down
his flank, a brief toss of his head to throw
a snort to catch the scent of you still there
beneath the stench of smouldering keratin.

And all the way back home the Old Horse
must have felt as if he was on stilts, while you
watched every footfall for its measured weight

That gave a grown-up lightness to your own.

Hard Done By

Great Grandpa took a strap to you
so often that poor Gran would
wring her own hands useless
all the while he would not stop and
one time, only a silent neighbour's
iron arm prevented damage being done.

So inches-wide that strap, so
many times whipped with a
snap from trouser loops – so
often did you take the blame for
cousins who had learned to curry favour
and delight in pulling from a hat

Your name – that one unhappy day
you ran away as far as you might
reasonably dare – down to the post box
with a letter for your mum to
ask her to get better soon, to

Come and take you home.

From your bare hand
I had one single, stinging smack
that snapped me to my senses
while my windbag howl
was lost, for you, at once,

Among the squealing
twist and turn of
proper cries above
Great Grandpa's shouts
set saucepan-clattering in your head.
I saw you turn your face away
to lose them where you could.

'I am hard-done-by – yes!' I dared
when I was fourteen and
for just a moment, all
that you could do was stare at me

In flashback and in disbelief.

You chased me round the kitchen table, then
until my panic and expostulation
weakened you with laughter
and you buckled at one knee
upon it, while I stood there,
opposite, hands loosening at my sides

Incredulous at my good fortune –

And your turning tide.

On the Promenade at Margate

(for Col & Dan)

You are a Man in miniature

(apart from the ears, that is)
buttoned, one side to the other
(to keep a growing lad in) socked,
to the scrubbed-potato knees, capped
so you wouldn't forget to be a
Monday schoolboy, still –

Catching the eye of a Sunday
photographer scuttling his tripod
to peg-down, at last, such a family,
taking the air off the sea or
churchgoing even – and proud
to be one of those families
just such a man with a camera
would recognise (making sure
not to walk past very fast).

Gramps to my own children.

(These are your Great Nan and
Great Grandad, too, snapped
on the promenade –
Possibly looking at you).

The Photo in the Drawer

In this photograph, Dad –
the one Our Mum cut off
to leave you in –

You are as old as my own Dan.

(He might have been some-
body playing the drums
at your Airforce dance
and you didn't even know.)

It feels like
I am father
to you both.

I want to protect you,
already – before
I am born –

From what
I know is
bound to be.

The Wrestling Field

Where there is an Outside Eating Area
(a beer garden par excellence)
across the road from where the
Village Inn has always been –

There was a wrestling field.

Where now are picnic tables,
with their parasols, in season,

Once upon a time you
wrestled with your father
in a milling, grassy space;
the 'mowey pastures' –
underneath the watchful eye
of 'sticklers' (referees, in
threes, with walking sticks
for separating, as and when)

The father reaching out a hand
(despite the arm-lock he was in)
to tag the son – the son

Quick-ducking ropes
to see the contest won.

Jack

Jack was your dad –
A coalminer Cornishman,
easy with us and

Easier, still, with you.
Ending your stories with
'Getaway! Getaway!'

Losing his voice
in the seams of his
cigarette smoke, coughing
deep in the pit of his
throat. Always
coming back up
for more –

Always about to say something
but letting us finish first –
leaving us wondering
quite what he thought we had meant.

Spreading the Marmite
so thick on his toast with his
daffodil pollen-stained fingers,
we looked at each other
and wondered if
someone should tell him

It wasn't the Chocolate Spread.

Circle for a Maid

(for my mother)

You couldn't quite believe
what you had come to. Dad
would not have said a great deal to
prepare you for it but at least you
understood, this early, that it
wasn't only him – that no-one
here had very much to say.

And so, by way of introduction,
(hardly an inspection – no-one
raised a sheepish eye from under-
neath a cap – inauguration, even)
everybody gathered, more or less
unbidden, on the hamlet green;

A dozen Cornishmen – reducing
such a thing, superfluous, as words, to
simple, bestial, amiable noises of
encouragement (or so you took it)
possibly approval (at a stretch); so

Soft and thickly-clotted, lilting-
pastoral, rhetorical – as if
you were but incidental and yet
instrumental in young Lawrie's
slight return. All taciturn

Among the chickens and the
milk churns on the steps. The

Cornish stone circles I took you to
a quarter of a lifetime on had
more to say! Boscawen, Hurlers (the),
Trevethy Quoit (not quite a circle),
Merry Maidens and the Nine
of them, of course, though

You the merriest that day.

Lol

Your baby brother, Howard
(known as Bill) still
calls you Lol. So Lol it is.

One day a convoy rumbled
past the house, transporting
R.A.F. recruits. 'Look – look!'
he cried, 'A lorryload of Lols!'

So Lol it is.

Four

Demob

You were variously

An Ice-cream Salesman
(on a tricycle with a big
refridgerated box for wafers,
cornets and six dozen
ice-cream bricks between
the two front wheels – which
must have been a Dickens
of a job to pedal, full of ice-
cream still, on rainy days, uphill),

A Gardener at a country house
(for which position's interview
you'd worn your best white gloves –
to demonstrate you knew
the gardening was well-to-do)

An Assistant Heating Engineer
(at the time when I was born – so
that is what is written that you
were upon my birth certificate)

A Steeplejack, of sorts, erecting
scaffolding round chimneys as they
nudged and wobbled to the sky –

For days and weeks and months
after the RAF had nothing
left for you to do – when all
you wanted was to be an
off-the-peg, in-uniform

Policeman; black for air-force blue –

The only life for you we ever knew.

One Moment

One moment . . .

You were holding me up
in the frame of the window
as if only yourself and
this child were in focus

To watch the marines, all
stamp-happy sailorly, on the
parade ground and wait
for the one on his own
by the flagpole to
play us the tune only
you knew the words for . . .

. . . *'the Mose , oh,*
the Mose, oh, the
Mose, oh, the Mose' . . .

To do with a cat
that turned up on the
doorstep after a storm

And the next . . .

I was flying along
the Kent coast road
beneath the cooling
towers that I never
dared look up at –

On the long-nosed bicycle seat
you'd spannered to the cross-bar
just enough to balance me
between your pumping knees –
with nothing for my hands to
do but fiddle with the yo-yo bell,
the rainy wind upon my face,
your big breath pedalling
in my ears – from Ramsgate

All the way to Deal.

All

I remember how
you always picked me up and

Always put me down again –
however small – with

All your strength.

Your strength

And all.

Point Duty

We only bumped into you twice
on Point Duty – out shopping in the
Town on Saturday – and you

Stood in the middle of the High Street
(in the days before such things as lights)
Directing traffic – one large

White-gloved hand, as if against a wall, to Halt.
The other beckoning those vehicles waiting, at a
quarter-turn – then 'face-about' in your
unflustered, own good time to give
those other John & Janet buses, lorries,
motorcycles, vans and cars their go.

It wasn't those blind gloves
which told of some emergency,
or even your policeman's helmet
(sure to biff my nose whenever
I was wearing it) the noisy,
engine-gathering enormity
of such responsibility – that
quietened me as we began to cross
the road with Mark sat in the
pushchair, down the kerb
and up at your behest:

It was your chin –
set firm against the
slightest smile – your
Bearskin sentry
undistractability
that wouldn't even
let you look at me.

Garages

Even at the time –

I wondered how it was that Christmas morning
I should have a wooden garage filled with Corgi cars
(still in their boxes which they don't do these days
but were like a little garage in themselves) while
Mark, who hankered for them every bit as much, though
three years younger, had a Matchbox Garage
(Matchbox being half the size with hardly any
die-cast details such as opening boots and bonnets).

Kneeling on the carpet ready for our transport of delight,
I looked at him but Mark seemed happy. Maybe it was
simply that the either end of those three years seemed
further separated by my own fortuitous head-start, to you,
than to ourselves, who only had our quarrelling to go by.

Then again, perhaps it said as much about your own
small-boyish thrill at week-by-week collecting one of each to
stack up on the tallboy top until we glimpsed the multi-storey
levels of those boxes building and could not believe our luck
(without a backward glance at Father Christmas)

Every whispered tucking of the box-flap back
(as if you'd caught yourself out peeping) making
all that extra shift work worth the while for
something like the nine whole months it took.

In Red

You underlined everything.

Every word was
underlined in red
until it said
what it already said.

My chin laid on the back of a chair
at the studying table, practising
your own tight lips and frown
without disturbing you
in any way at all, I

Was very glad to notice
that the Law was good

Because you were a policeman
and that you agreed
with nearly all of it,
at least, in red.

Fingerprints

You were a specialist
in Scenes of Crime
and Fingerprints.

We learned them, too;
whorl and double-loop
and bifurcated arch –

Sat, close-for-comfort
with you, fascinated
by each shoelace-loopy
intimacy that would
nose up underneath the
one above and make it
topple over, rather like
your own wry eyebrows
that we liked to watch.

We traced along them,
wanting them to be
a proper maze as if
this was a puzzle book.
There never was a
satisfactory solution
to those fingerprints. We

Understood that you could
easily identify a person
by a single fingerprint, that
you could tell a good man
from a bad one, though it
wasn't by their type of
pattern – which I never
fathomed. When you

Frowned, I didn't know
if it was that you didn't
want us touching
bad men's fingerprints
because they might be
touching us as well, or
whether it was time for you
to concentrate. We were still

Learning to identify you properly.

My Dad's a Policeman

Was my standard response
to being in trouble,
as if I couldn't possibly be
if you were –
or at least, you'd
get me out of it –
if I was.

Half an Ounce of Old Holborn

Half a crown closed tight in a fist.
'Half an Ounce of Old Holborn – as
soon as you like.'

I imagined the green and the gold,
the way the tobacco would
squash in its packet, ran to

The newsagents, practising
what I would say. At the bottom
of Nethercourt Hill I remembered
I hadn't seen Dad's half a crown

Since he'd pressed it there,
heavy and milled, thumb to the
back of it, into the
well of my palm – and
opened my hand up to
see it. The half a crown

Stuck for a moment –
sweated to skin, then

Dropped – out through the grab of
my suddenly straw-clutching fingers and
bounced on the grill of a
drain by the side of the road,

Slipped – with a silvery wink
between ironwork bars-of-a-prison
which bit me a groove in the back of
my hand as it jammed
and it jammed. I

Listened, in horror, for the sound
of its big, fruity plop, Sank
to my knees in the gravel and
desperately tried to imagine
myself at the newsagents shop.

Time and again I
tried to go home but
returned to the drain, til
I knew Dad would know
I should have been
back long ago – so

I stood at the
living-room door.
Dad had a visitor –
someone from work.
A policeman like him,
who probably already knew.

'Dad' –

'Not now, Son.'

'That half a crown' –

'What did I say to you? Pardon?
Never you mind, Sonny Jim –
I shan't tell you again.'

Halfway upstairs
I stopped and I turned.
They were laughing.

I couldn't believe
they were laughing
when here I was – yet
to be called to account

For the no Half an Ounce of
Old Holborn as well as the

No half a crown –
down the drain.

Cornwall

Holidays in Cornwall
were not many,
though they
counted themselves
annually, as you

Talked them up –
until we quite believed
we'd been that year
when it appeared
we'd not. The

Clotted cream and
cow pat smell of it
was there the moment
you allowed the
words *Polzeath, Port
Isaac and Trequite*
to pass your lips – the

Room was hushed at
once. You named them
reverently with Rs
rolled from some
Merlin-magic
alphabet. We

Started longing for the
journey straightaway –
though it would take
from one end of the
day until the other –

So that even when the
windscreen shattered
just this side of Saltash
(inauspiciously, the
year the Tamar Bridge
was opened – 1961)

And I was laying all
along the back seat
with the Whooping
Cough and coat and
blanket on, I could not

Stop imagining the
milk churns and the
milling chickens and the
farmyard gate and
Auntie Dot already
there to open it

On two, or maybe
three occasions,
anyway.

Pickled Onions

Somehow it didn't surprise us one bit
that the bedroom airing-cupboard (and
supposedly, our toy cupboard as well)

Was just the place to keep your pickled onions;

Glassy-shouldered storage jars that
vied for space astride the wooden slats, all
full of prize and as yet pale, green onions, blind
from the garden earth, with little red and yellow,
moon-curled spices (which, I guess, were chillies)
doing what they could to float between them and
the most exotic evidence of other worlds we
ever saw inside the house – each jar-neck

Ear-drummed tight with greaseproof paper and
elastic-banded half a dozen times to
seal the onions in and seal us out.

You'd see how they were doing; give
each jar a quarter-turn before you
came to plant a forehead kiss goodnight
while we were reading comics and
would not have necessarily looked up.

We always knew when you'd been on a 2 to 10
and come upstairs, police-boot socked,
to see your pickled onions one last time
because there'd be a Bandit chocolate bar
upon each bedside chair, there, in the morning

And the pickled onions hadn't yet been stolen.

On Sweltering Days

On sweltering days like these
when the sky was grey with heat
and leaves turned soft and
garden turf was only crumbly soil
with stiff little hay for grass, when
everybody's bare backs, even in the
house, were sticking to their chairs –

You would reach for the
kitchen-door handle that squeaked,
in your shiny-blue, boxing-ring shorts
and a spring in your barefoot step

And go for the hottest, most un-shady
part of the afternoon oven, to turn
from your back to your front on a towel
and invent us a new shade of creosote.

In you would come, basted,
glistening, marinaded in sweat, a
maraschino grin. *'It's just a
trifle warm out there –'*
you'd let us know and then

You would cool yourself down
with your face to the white
of the ceiling, fogged in the smoke
of an Old Holborn weed.

At the Crease

July was your time.

At the close of its long summer days
you would stand at the crease
at the top of the Corgi-car slope,
defending the front-garden gate
and its dustbin-lid wicket –
a child's bat in hand and

Keep all-comers out.

Friends in the road would be
fielding all over the garden, big
boys that we hardly knew
would come, hesitant, in
through the double-gates
meant for the car and would
try to dispatch you, to catch
you, then slope off – their
heads bobbing over the wall.

Come winter; one such
when a continent's snow had
been dumped at the front-door
to muffle the letter-box,
taunt us with snow-pipes
the shape of the milk-bottle
'empties' we took in again –
you would scrape with a
a spade at the concrete to
clear us a bobsleigh-run
ready for school and
then drag the gate open
to stand at the crease,

Inviting our snowballs
to clomp with the spade
til the path needed
scraping all over again.

Night Fishing

(to Howard)

How hard could it be?
This fishing lark –
this food for free
when we lived by
the jolly sea?
Especially at night
when fish weren't
going to see what
not to bite. You

Turned up at the harbour wall
just as the other fishermen were
going home – with little brother,
Howard, who might think himself a
fisherman but whom you'd show
a thing or two before the night was out –
the pair of you upon your bicycles, two
hand-lines and a jar of ragworm bait.

You whirled the baited lines around
your heads to clear the wall,
then settled down to wait.

No fish. You dragged the lines
back up the wall a dozen times.
No ragworm either – so yet more
such gruesome, evil-smelling,
un-compliant horrors to be pinched
and hooked until the last one and
the fattest and the leggiest of all
fell in your lap and you effected
to secure it to your flies – then
cried with laughter at your
new appendage. Come the

Dawn, you thought to look
over the harbour wall at last
and found the tide was out;
There'd been no sea at all
throughout the night while
harbour crabs enjoyed your
ragworms out of sight. The

Two of you were far too weak
with all your laughing at each other
to get on your bikes – so
wheeled them home,
inebriated with your
foolishness. No promised

Fish for breakfast. Mark
and I stood in the kitchen
none the wiser. What was
Uncle Howard doing here
and with his bicycle to
have to pedal thirteen miles
back home to Deal to
do his paper-round? He
chuckles at it even now.

How Men Run

We found a lizard, hot
among the summer legs
and ankle socks and
spinny pushchair wheels
upon our way to the
Policemen's Sports.
It would not leave
the heat of its own
stone upon the path –
still wanting any sun
that made the car roofs
colourful – its head all
paved with fingernails
of hexagon. Up on

The inchworm hump
of the bridge I could
suddenly see those all-
too newly-laundered
running lines – bird-
dropping white. My
small heart thumped
at the confinement of
those tracks that wound
and wound like bandages,
like chalky plaster-casts,
with nowhere to get off.

I looked at you but you
were only walking still and
in your shirt and trousers
though you grinned at me
your tight-lipped grin for
keeping all the worries in.
We found a family spot
of sun-browned grass
too close, I thought, to the
stiff, white grass of the
outside lane. I looked again
and you were gone.

After a bang – Men Ran;
their faces angry with
themselves – not looking
to see if their arms and legs
were still their own or not.

I did not realise that bodies
could be such machinery and
every moment such a perfect
copy of the one before.
Not one of them was you.

Until I saw you coming –
last of all, around the bend,
not straight and tall but
leaning over like a
motorcycle rider –
Trying to catch up.

I called out 'Dad!' then
quickly stepped back
at the working of you, at
the thud of you upon the
ground, the wobble of your
muscles and the blow of air
push-pushed just like the
steam-hiss from a train,
your eyebrows knit into a
coal-black V and not a
moment spare to even
glance this way, at me.

And when you found us,
dressed as our own Dad,
you laughed and told us
how the man who'd passed
the relay baton to you had
gasped 'sorry, mate' – and
then I knew you'd had to run
much more than anyone
and still come, was it third?
I think you said. I

Wasn't listening by then –
just wishing I could
see you do all that again.

Still Life with Apples

Here we are with Uncle John's new Mini
on the cliffs at Dover, at-a-slope down to that
big white chalky drop into the Channel
with an apple – Granny Smiths, it looks like;

Offspring of your very own, encouraged,
no doubt fondly, for the camera by Auntie Ruth and
you – out of your comfort zone in any case – now
wondering what possible use, the oldest one,
making his face like that, might turn out to be.

The car is warm on our backs in the sun
though the windows aren't wound down.
I wonder why not. Mum looks young enough
to be somebody's sister. Uncle John's
I would imagine. You are just as

I remember you; only one bite from your apple
with always about to say something to me
that might make a blind bit of difference –

Finding it hard to do this Still Life.

Stand Up Straight

You gave me a life and a
brown paper bag with a
talent or two that
neither of us took to
looking in much –

You weren't very big
on the Use It or Bury
And Lose It. You

Let my childhood be;
made only one demand
of me (apart from
emptying my plate)

That I should
Jolly-well
(and quick
about it,
Laddie)

Stand up
straight.

Dave Allen

You saw yourself
up on that infamous stool,

flicking invisible ash
from your knee,

holding the whiskey glass
everyone knew

was just full of the Irish for water.
Not ruffled at all, but for the

hand through the hair.
Taking you into his confidence

so that, cannily cynical, too,
you were laughing your way to the

punchline he never did need –
when an eye might be widened,

or cast, with a twinkle,
towards the Almighty,

or fingers unfurled
from a supplicant palm
on the point of an elbow

for want of an answer at all.

PEO – PLE

I learned it like that – with a gap –
whilst walking round and round the
living-room, to your own rhythm;

PEO-PLE. You were not pleased.
My school report had said I never
came out well in Spelling Tests.
You'd no idea. And Parents Evening
was still worse. (The only one you
ever went to, such was the
resounding ignominy)

So you made a music out of it –
and you were right. It's how I still

Remember how to spell the lot of us correctly –

And perhaps how words became
so personable and so full of song for me.

The Sniff

Elbow to elbow.
Bone-stones
on the table top.

Arms locked at the hand –
with your Big Man's one
bending double at the wrist
accommodating yet another
small contender's grip. Then

'Sorry? Have you started yet?'
You'd ask, while we'd been
straining at you for a minute
and you hadn't even noticed –
Both hands now then,
on our feet and all our
weight across the table
at your tree-trunk, fence-post,
maypole (others dancing
round it, gleeful) forearm.

Any moment now.
'No, no – don't do it, Dad!'
Your eyes are widening.
It's on its way. It's coming.
'Dad – not yet, not yet!
Please – please!'
Oh, any moment now –

The Sniff.

And there it was.
All over. One arm
flat upon the table
lost to sight beneath the

Other. So 'Not Fair.'
With all your great big muscles –
still you had to go and do
The Sniff.

Playing Table Tennis

The point was – you would win.
We never thought about it twice.
However many points we played to;
21 – or *'just a quick one to 11, then'* –

You won because no other outcome was
Conceivable. And then, when I was 17,
I almost got away with the unthinkable –

You only beat me 21-19. I saw
You felt you'd been betrayed

The very last time that we played.

Nine Card Brag

With Noel, born on Christmas Day
(while Mark and I were reading
Dandy or the Beano, downstairs)

You had met your match.

No doubt that you would win
hand after hand after hand of the
card games you taught us;
Rummy and Whist and the
evergreen Nine Card Brag –
with pack after pack in the
post for a year in exchange
for the Old Holborn wrappers
we made sure you sent off –

But Noel would not let you
get away lightly, with something
so easy as winning. It was always –

'Just one more game, Dad –
one more game. Go on, Dad,
go on – Oh, come on, Dad.
Thanks Dad. Last one, then –
Dad. Just one more game!'

Til, single-handedly, he
wore you down and finally
the winning was not nearly
so important as the losing.

I would hang about around the
edges of such marathons –
amazed at your eventual and
almost pitiable come-uppance.

A Certain Age

i

When I was at that certain age –
you always came in
too late for the boiler
by the back door
to kick up a greeting,

Letting in more than a foot-in-the-doorway
of your own dark – not ours, policeman's dark –
to trouble the kitchen with chills in the

Serge of your uniform still,
and a faint must of
bad men and places.

The doorstep itself would trip the
throaty jolt of recognition from you
that I counted on; 'All right, then?'
or the short, pre-occupied, 'Uh –huh?'
I had no answer to at all – the

Neither of them lost upon me in amongst
your big coat-carcass shruggings-off, the
podding of your feet to the dullest of drum-rolls
onto the doormat. Both, though,

Strained with puzzlement or spiced with
a sniff of amusement

At the finding of me here again.

ii

Eyes gaslit in the grey face, then and
turned up wide in order
to extract one last confession – the
whistle and the steam to which
I would be proudly witness.

By default, the two of us,
a silent-movie double-act -
Unlikely – in the

Spotlight-squares of all the
country-music-coloured kitchen cupboards
(glossy red and yellow, black – the
colours that you liked to like).

Tinned-milk and tea leaves
left to stew, three sugars, while,
with eyelids closing
to the back of teaspoons –
nicotine and petrol seasoned profile tipped
a moment to the ceiling at the

Draining-board – you
registered me with a
tea-bag squeeze of smile, and
with a bang of pedal-bin
I dropped into your motoring,
down to idling, mind.

                        iii

Until the Roman-glassy television
pulled a windflash crackle
'cross the screen into a
lightbulb tinkle and an
Adam's apple thump – and
blessed your cigarette smoke
with its clammy moonlight,

Eased your temples from your fingertips
by swapping consciousnesses for you;
Robbers and Cops for
Cops and Robbers. You
basking in the glare, me,
sipping-sidekick in the shadows.

Weighty minutes
tipped one day
into the next – to
leave you lightened,
somehow, and relieved
of old responsibilities.

'Drop more milk, I think –'
You got up, grinning at me
and the furniture slid into place.

I could leave you safely now to Sportsnight
and look forward to cheers and
commentary upon you through the
bedroom wall, anticipate
that I might fall asleep
before you snapped the light
behind the kitchen door.

iv

I would have charmed you back again,
however late at night,
whichever shift you might have been on –
point you to the kettle
in my own small kitchen, but

I could not find a storyline
to spark your vital interest
in later episodes of me

And it is no-one else but me that rinses out the mug
and pulls the plug and lets the dog out
one last time – who listens for his own small children
in their own, familiar, darknesses.

The key turns noisily tonight
as if to let me know for sure

That there is no-one left

When I have gone upstairs.

Out on a Limb

I went out on a limb –
left home to prove
to anybody listening
that I could –

Kept coming back
to see how everybody was,
to ask if there were any little
jobs that needed doing –

Spent the odd night
on the living-room settee.

One such, you came in
from one more 2 to 10
and found me there,
not quite asleep.

You sat at the end
by my two crossed feet.
*'You can always come home
if you need to, Old Son.'*

'Thanks, Dad. I know,'
I said, thought 'maybe
this is the moment to
do Dad the courtesy of
actually telling him I had
left home in the first place.'

I didn't. You got up.
We skirted the
settee some more.

Blackberries

Bending to blackberries.

Fingertip practised
and sprightly for ever-
so-lightly enticing a
grand-daughter's words
from her thoughts without
risking their squashing
or bruising (such care
in their choosing) – the
juice of them staining the
moments remaining – and
dropping them, plump
and un-plopping now into the
ice-cream container, the
both of you keeping an
eye on their piling; their
volcano rolling-beguiling
that might be escaping –

Your heads gravitating
around your soft harvesting –

Here in these overgrown
Edgbaston gardens, the
houses demolished,
returning to wilderness –

Somewhere to take our
own purple-moon visitors.

Company Man

Your services were required
all over the place. Indispensable
again. In a Company car.
Your own man at last.

We would meet between offices;
pin in the map between Cambridge
and Peterborough. You left it
for me to decide. I surprised us.
Emily's Wood – which you'd
never heard of (while deep down
I still believed there wasn't
anything you didn't know) and
here it was me arranging the thing;

Where to meet, deciding
that we should meet, even –
after all this time. (Had you
been waiting for me to
'show some initiative' as
if there was a school report
still running?) I knew

You'd have to acquiesce
in some way I was not
yet clear about, to
years I had accumulated
(two or three to every
one of yours) – to give the
weight of them their due.
I was a man with family,
with children that would
give me ballast in your
company and a career
which paid the mortgage.
(You had always said you
had no fears as far as that
might be concerned. It
seemed a cop-out at the time.)

I recognised you. You had
found another turning-circle
on the wide grass verge
along the forest road. I
think we both made quite a
show of locking cars
and pocketing the keys

And there it was – your
Appalachian smile,
your stepping over
puddles and through
sticks, assured – to

Draw our greetings

Get us going for our
grins and hugs and
not a year too soon.

A rite of passage on
our naff High Noon.

Shallows

One day I came to see you
renovate this cottage that you
always talked about –

See it for myself, see
where you'd found your
way back to, exactly. So

You cleared your throat and
smiled and put things down
to show me round the bendy stairs
and fireplaces, nooks and little
cubbyholes you peered into
as if we'd just discovered them
together. I inquired if

You remembered it
from when you were a boy.
You weren't inclined to answer.

I had made-believe that if, today,
you chose to drive us through the
village ford, your childhood lanes
would open up for both of us –
that this would be a light and
shallow baptism; a happy shock of
cold and wet that would invigorate us
evermore – new father and new son –

While what I came away with
was another version of your
quick-flash smile as you
changed gear – which

Didn't seem so sacred at the time
though now, of course, it
scarifies my soul.

Four Sons

(for Luke)

You had four sons;

Two while you were young,
with whom you grew up wondering
just what you'd taken on,

One, when you were not so young,
who took care of our mother for you
when your mind and body told you
two halves do not always make a whole

And one when you were older still
who had no problem with the idea of
the sum of all such parts

And simply would not let this be.

Creases

So here it was – your piece of Cornwall.

Where you fell off the roof
in some surprise at seeing Mum one day – the
last place you'd expected – where the

Ship's own timber hid behind the
plaster of the chimney breast
caught, slowly fire, glowed orange
through it, three whole days,
where one son and his own

Made hay for you, up to their elbows
in the so-called garden all that summer.
(Oh, how many gardens well begun then,
wanton, let return to wilderness) Where was

The cottage you were left with
when the market bottomed-out
with you still decorating and that
nobody would buy at any price
no matter how you lowered it or
creased the map still more with
complimentary trips to show
prospective buyers what they
should, undoubtedly, be missing –

Where you would have started up again, found
yet another place for sale, got
back up off the floor like Henry Cooper
(I remember how you couldn't help
the sharp intakes of breath yourself
with Conteh or McGuigan on the telly),
smiled at the suggestion of a blow
to body or to head that might be
landed well enough to punch out
your longstanding Cornish dream.

It wasn't punches. It was creases;
Illness you could never have imagined

Folding you into yourself; a life
mapped-out to several scales that
did not think to fit – and folded smaller
and then smaller and yet smaller still.

Toughening Up

(your R.A.F. photograph)

It's you, all right, though

Not in the policeman's
uniform we understood
you in and Mum ironed
all those dark-blue shirts

For. It is you
but so far back
you haven't even
learned to fly

Or catch somebody
else's eye. A
thumping-
hearted
youngster,
trying to set
a soft face hard.

Choosing a manhood.
Closing your eyes and
jumping in with both feet
so you'd have to learn to swim.

This was the way to toughen-up:
You let the Forces have you
(while you drove munitions lorries
through the luke-warm dregs of war).

It wasn't as if you needed
toughening-up again
and when the doctor
dipped his finger
in the shadow of your eyelid

He took pains to tell us
that whatever you
had dragged yourself
through this time

Your heart was
like an ox's. It
was all the rest.